ALCOHOLISM

ALCOHOLISM
HOW TO FULLY RECOVER AND LIVE LIFE MORE ABUNDANTLY

ANTHONY PARKER

iUniverse, Inc.
New York Lincoln Shanghai

ALCOHOLISM
HOW TO FULLY RECOVER AND LIVE LIFE MORE ABUNDANTLY

iUniverse books may be ordered through booksellers or by contacting:

iUniverse
2021 Pine Lake Road, Suite 100
Lincoln, NE 68512
www.iuniverse.com
1-800-Authors (1-800-288-4677)

Because of the dynamic nature of the Internet, any Web addresses or links contained in this book may have changed since publication and may no longer be valid.

ISBN: 978-0-595-49683-9 (pbk)
ISBN: 978-0-595-61208-6 (ebk)

Printed in the United States of America

To all those who have gone through; and are now going through the battle of alcoholism. Take it one day at a time and have faith that there is abundant life after the storm. You just have to believe.

Contents

ACKNOWLEDGMENTS

I acknowledge that God has kept me and blessed me so that I can be a voice and save His beloved children from the destruction of Alcoholism.

To my mother: Annette and step-father, the late Bennett Thompson, I love you. Thank you!

To my father Jobie: it was your early teachings that helped me to reach this abundant life I now have.

To my wonderful children: I love you with all my heart. You help to make this abundant life worth living. Jessica thanks for being there from the start.

To my sisters: Renea Marrow and Yvette Parker. I love you dearly. Yvette thanks for inspiring and motivating me to live a better life. It worked … and I love it!

To Brenda Faye: thank you for your kindness, support, and everlasting friendship.

To Gregory and Eureka Collins: thank you for your untiring love and guidance. You have been an inspiration in my life and I sincerely thank you. The two of you are not only fellow authors, but the definition of a great marriage bond. You both have inspired me.

To all of my family and friends (too many to name): I love you dearly. Thank you for not giving up on me and loving me in spite of myself.

FOREWORD

In this breakthrough book, Anthony Parker has opened his life to the public. He has invited you to share in a life of abundance. As you read the following pages, you will find that his life was filled with trials and tribulations, much attributed to drinking alcohol.

No man can be blamed for trying to fool other people about himself. After all, that is the way most people live; but what can be said for a man who tries to fool himself? Every man knows exactly how bogus he is and should admit it to himself. The man who, knowing his bogusness, refuses to admit it to himself no matter what his attitude may be to the outside world simply stores up trouble and discomfort for himself. There are many phases of personal understanding of one-self that need not be put in the newspapers or proclaimed publicly.

When it comes to fooling oneself by oneself, the greatest performers are those who have a habit no matter what kind of a habit! It may be smoking cigarettes, or walking pigeon-toed, or talking through the nose, or drinking or anything else. Any alcoholic can see with half an eye opened how drinking is hurting someone else; but always argues that his or her own personal drinking is of a different variety and is doing him or her no harm.

That is the reason drinking alcohol destroys so many people either by wrecking their health or by attaching on them the habit they cannot stop. They fool themselves. They are perfectly well aware that others are drinking too much but not themselves. Far be it from them not to have the will-power to stop when it is time to stop. They are smarter than their neighbors. They know what they are doing. And suddenly the explosions come!

There are hundreds of thousands of men and women in all walks of life in this country who for twenty or thirty years have never lived a minute when there was not more or less alcohol in their systems. They cannot be said to have been strictly and entirely sober in all that time, but who do their work, perform all their social duties, maintain their careers and are fairly successful just the same.

There has been more information printed and spoken about drinking alcohol than about any other employment, avocation, vocation, habit, practice or pleasure of mankind. However, none of them are as life changing as this book. Drinking alcohol is a personal proposition—a choice.

The *choice* to drink alcohol is frequently neither more nor less than an evil trick or habit, whose very charm and influence over its ill-fated slave depend upon its continuity from day to day, or from hour to hour. If this continuity can be interrupted for a sufficient time, a healthier moral action supervenes. The charm is broken and the intemperate is awakened to a new code of sensations from the tears of joy, which are shed around him, he gathers the conviction that he is not utterly despised. The neglected wife or husband dares to hope for brighter days, children shake off their terror and climb once more on the parent's knee, and God safeguards a smile of approbation. The poor, pitiable alcoholic gathers up the fallen respectability and takes a new departure for the voyage of life. Yes, the alcoholic becomes a faithful and affectionate spouse, and a child of God. Therefore, take the principles in this book, apply them, and live the rest of your life more abundantly.

Gregory Collins
Author, The Radiant Powers of Success

INTRODUCTION

People who do not drink are not only happier, healthier, and able to earn more money, but their home and family are also benefited. The homes of such people are orderly and well conducted. It is well furnished and has an air of comfort and prosperity. Both spouses and their family are comfortable, contented, and valuable citizens of the State. They save their money, and when it has to be spent, it is spent wisely. Such people practice thrift.

Thrift means a state of thriving. We can all understand what this means. When we say that a plant or animal is thriving we mean that it is growing and developing. If it is not doing this, then there is something wrong. Persons and families that practice thrift are in a state of thriving. Thrift is generally applied to saving money, and in order to save money we must exercise care in spending it. Thrift is the opposite of waste, and just as alcohol is the main cause of waste, so it is the main enemy of thrift. The people who do not waste their money on alcohol can save a large sum by the end of the year. They can put their money in the bank so that it may be useful to them on some future occasion when needed. They may spend it wisely in food or clothing. In this way, they benefit by their thrift and are better off. The family shares these benefits along with them.

Everyone should practice thrift, both children and grown-up people. This does not mean that they should be mean, greedy or selfish. There is a great difference between greed, selfishness and true thrift.

No one should waste either money or anything else. It is the duty of everyone to practice thrift and to try to get others to practice it also.

In the sober home, the children are well cared for. They have plenty of suitable food to build up their bodies and to give them energy for their work and play. They are well clothed, therefore in cold weather their bodies are kept warm, and they are therefore able to resist the attack by the germs of disease. The children of sober parents are generally better educated. If they wish to learn anything for which a special training is necessary they can obtain this. They are able to get into good situations and to be happy and successful in their later life. They learn to be thrifty and careful, as well as to avoid the waste and danger caused by alcohol. Like their parents they also become valuable citizens.

If sober parents should by some misfortune, for which they have no responsibility, lose their employment for a time or suffer from some unavoidable accident, then they are able to meet their ill-fortune with the resources supplied by their thrifty and careful habits. They can use the money that they have saved to cover times of difficulty. Often such people belong to a "society" of those like themselves who are careful to provide for times of difficulty. They pay so much a week or a month, and in sickness or other difficulty they have a nice sum to help them during the time when they are unable to work. All young persons when they are old enough should be taught to save portions of their money to help them during temporary hardship or misfortune. In many cases, a sum of money is invested for retirement age. All these benefits are more commonly enjoyed by those who do not waste their money on alcohol.

If people waste their money on alcohol they do not injure themselves only, but also all those who are connected to them or depend on them in any way. Alcohol is the enemy of the family. It destroys comfort, that is to say, it alters the condition of affairs which permits a family to provide for all its daily needs: food, clothing, lodging, fire, light, etc. Let us say that a man does not spend his earnings on each of these necessities of life, then his wife and children have to go without them, fall into debt or seek assistance from charity. Moreover, the people who waste their money on alcohol are unable to make any provision for the future. They do not save anything, they put no money in the bank, and they do not join their sober and thrifty co-workers in investing for the future. Therefore, when they are out of work, the victims of sickness or accident, they are unable to do anything to meet their difficulties.

The money that people waste on alcohol is lost, because they do not receive a proper return for it. At the end of each year they are poorer by the amount they have spent, without any increase in health, strength or comfort. On the contrary, they are probably worse off in all these particulars. They may not be a drunkard or even a regular drinker. But even if they spent a small part of their money on drink they will have to spend less on something else. They will buy less food or clothing, and yet their family will be hungry and insufficiently clothed.

The habits of drinkers affect their spouse and children. The home is torn and unhappy. There is not sufficient money to buy food and clothes or other things which produce comfort and increase the pleasure of life. Those who suffer most are the spouse and children, and they often have a miserable and unhappy life. Sometimes both parents are drinkers, and then the children are neglected, and in many cases even treated with cruelty. They have no chance of making a good start in life. They are not properly fed, and their health and energy are below the average. They do not grow in the same way as children who are properly fed and carefully looked after, and they cannot learn their school lessons so well as their brains are not properly nourished. Such children become accustomed to poverty and discomfort and they grow up without any desire to do any better themselves. Often, indeed, they learn to drink while quite young. They are injured from the start in both body and mind, and their chances of leading happy and useful lives are greatly lessened. Of course, this is not the exact measurements of all situations but is common in most.

Alcohol destroys the whole family life. Affection and respect for one another disappear. There are quarrels, threats, and often fighting.

The children have a bad example always before them; they lose respect for their parents' authority and refuse to obey them. The parents waste their money, become cruel, neglect the children and often expose their lives to great risks. The drinker's home is the home of misery.

Some people who have not studied the question very carefully say that the reason people drink is because they are poor, ignorant, and miserable; and have to live in disgusting environments. This is not wholly true. The opposite is more often the truth. It is because they drink that they are poor, miserable and in distress. We know this because whenever these people get more money, instead of using it to make their homes more comfortable they spend it on more drink. Drink causes poverty far more often than poverty causes drink.

It is important to know this, because it explains why many efforts to improve the lot of the poor often fail. When people have acquired the habit of drinking, more prosperity means greater waste. Even when they earn higher wages, for a time, they spend more, and in the end are worse off than ever. Poverty will always exist as long as alcohol can be easily obtained.

Alcohol is intoxicating; that is people drink it. Those who find at the root of intoxication its pleasure and pain, its peril and penalty must study the physiological effects of alcohol on the brain. There they may read its story and its mystery. It is the beginning of the entire problem and no matter how much one blames matters on civics and economics.

This is the significant fact people have to set down against any gain from alcohol. It is understood that they are not interested in the person with the broken down liver and the rundown drunkard who has reached the end of his or her career. But take the ounce or two-a-day drinker who can drink and appear to be sober. Sobriety is a broad word. It includes the three planes. The body may be sober that is, normal enough; the emotional level, the imagination, even the higher intelligence, may be unaffected and unimpaired; but of no man, in whose bodily system there is alcohol in any degree, can it be said that his moral qualities are normal. Good conduct, like every other mental habit, must have an organic basis a mechanism of nerve-cells and fibers. This mechanism, as you know, is recently acquired in man and is still unstable and of extreme fragility. The alcohol which leaves the rest of the man "sober," beats savagely upon this fragile mechanism. Not perhaps, but certainly; not occasionally, but always. The first impairment is moral; the first lapse is moral; for every man who takes alcohol is drunk at the top.

This degeneration may not immediately express itself in immoral action; but you have only to wait. The moment the higher intelligence is touched in its turn by the toxic paralysis when the judgment goes off guard, and the emotions are uncontrolled that man will break the moral law. You can trust him neither with a purse or a woman or an oath. And if you are that man, you cannot trust yourself. You are drunk at the top. And so long as you drink you can not get morally sober, no matter how well in hand you keep mind and body. Every successive dose of alcohol goes there first. And every toxic repetition increases the moral disaster. No matter how sober he may be from that highest plane downward, the man who drinks alcohol is morally defective; he may keep within the criminal law because his judgment tells him to, or because his passions do not tempt him out of it; but morally he is impotent the very organic basis of altruism and good moral feeling in him is destroyed. It is dead of alcoholic paralysis.

Set that down in your account of profit and loss.

Do the gains seem especially attractive now you know the physiological price the mere destruction of the nerve-elements you are called upon to pay?

Alcohol ruins the home and through it injures the nation. It brutalizes men and degrades women and children. A house in which alcohol is used is in danger of ceasing to be a home.

Does that strike a responsive chord? Home is the place where men and women are trained and the nation is molded. A home which is prosperous and comfortable produces good citizens. A family that prays together will surely stay together.

God will enter when we open the door by implicit trust and takes up His abode with us and in us. By shedding abroad His love He quickens our whole souls into sympathy with Himself, and in this way, and in this way alone, He purifies our hearts through faith. He sustains our will in the attitude of devotion. He quickens and regulates our affections, desires, appetites and passions, and becomes our sanctification.

The Bible teaches that by trusting in Christ we receive an inward influence that stimulates and directs our activity; that by faith we receive His purifying influence into the very centre of our being; that through and by His truth revealed directly to the soul He quickens our whole inward being into the attitude of a loving obedience; and this is the way, and the only practicable way, to overcome alcoholism.

Those who possess such homes value them above everything on earth; when they have to leave them they do so with sorrow and regret and they look forward eagerly to their return. When they grow up and have homes of their own they try to model these on that in which they were brought up. Every home like this forms part of the national wealth.

If we begin to look through the eyes of our Creator, we will see that the world is good. We, being in and of the world, have a right to enjoy it, not in the old animal and sensual way, by abandoning ourselves to the lusts of the flesh, but in that temperate way which brings abundant life.

1

ALCOHOL AND THE
FAMILY

As you may recall in my Introduction, I stated, "Alcohol destroys the whole family life. Affection and respect for each other disappear. There are quarrels, threats, and often fighting. The children have a bad example always before them; they lose respect for their parents' authority and refuse to obey them. The parents waste their money, become cruel and neglect the children and often expose their lives to great risks. The drinker's home is the home of misery."

Well, I would like to fully illustrate its meaning, thereby I present this story:

There was a man named Seth Pearson who was in the United States Navy. During Veteran's Day weekend of 1999, his ship pulled in for a port visit. Seth and his friends were eagerly waiting for the taste of an ice cold beer and to listen to some music. Seth knew (or thought he knew) how to handle his booze. After all, he was the command's Drug and Alcohol Program Advisor.

Seth and his friends stopped at the first pub in their path. After a few hours of drinking beer after beer, they decided it was time to go to the local club. The group of friends was having a great time stumbling and staggering down the street. Once inside the club, they continued their alcohol indulgence. Seth glanced near the entrance of the club and saw two women standing there having a good time. One of the women seemed to have had a few drinks and was really letting her hair down. This attracted Seth and he decided to ask her to dance. Seth's friend, Dave, asked the other woman. Things hit off right from the start as alcohol was the driving force of the chance meeting.

While dancing, Seth asked what his partner's name was. "Chelsea," she replied. Dave found out that his dance partner's name was Amy. Around midnight, Seth and three of his friends along with Chelsea and Amy departed the club for a walk on the beach. Driven by the alcohol, all of them went for a dip in the cold water, although some of Seth's friends were not good swimmers. After their "polar plunge" they sat laughing on the beach. It was then that Seth and Chelsea started to converse more intimately and felt some chemistry between them.

Seth and Dave left the beach and went with Chelsea and Amy. The two couples caught a taxi to Chelsea's father's condominium. Upon arrival, Seth noticed something strange. Chelsea started yelling and screaming for unknown reasons. It was about 3:00 a.m. and Seth was standing there totally embarrassed. He got back into the cab and returned to the ship. Many thoughts crossed Seth's mind as he sat in the back of the cab. What had just happened? Chelsea appeared to have been a totally different person who Seth had enjoyed earlier. How could someone have changed so quickly when things seem to be going so well? And should he have left Dave at the condominium by himself? Then he remembered Amy had not been drinking as much as everyone else. Dave would call and check in he thought.

Seth arrived at the ship and all the while asking himself how could a person change so quickly. Was this just an isolated incident or is this the real individual? He said a prayer and went to sleep.

Suddenly, there was a knock on the door. Someone had a message for Seth to call Dave. Seth dressed himself and went to make the call. Dave answered the telephone and informed Seth that he was well. He also mentioned that Chelsea wanted Seth to meet her at the club later that evening. Reluctantly, Seth agreed to meet them later that evening.

Later that day, as agreed, Seth made his way to the club to meet Dave, Amy and Chelsea. The thoughts of Chelsea's early morning *temper tantrum* kept running through his mind. His gut feeling was telling him that being there was a big mistake. His upbringing within the church had much to do with his convictions. Since Seth had not made a life commitment to God, he continued his journey through the doors of the club. He saw Dave, Amy and Chelsea sitting at a table near the dance floor. During the initial greetings (and the apologies), a round of drinks arrived. Not realizing at the time, alcohol would become the focal point of the next few years of Dave's life.

The night went as the previous night with plenty of drinking alcohol without any cares or worries whatsoever. After a few hours of drinking alcohol and dancing, the four of them left to go to another club to continue their long night of partying. Dave mentioned that Chelsea had had too much to drink. She slipped, fell down and bruised her knee. Everyone shrugged it off because she was drunk and felt no pain.

Once more, the couples ended their night of drinking alcohol and dancing at Chelsea's father's condominium. That night began a new chapter in Seth's life. He and Chelsea engaged in sexual intercourse. Afterwards, Seth was thinking of him being raised in the Church and knowing right from wrong. However, the alcohol consumption pushed him into dreamland.

The next morning, the four of them woke up to massive hangovers. They agreed to cure their hangovers with Bloody Mary cocktails. Drinking alcohol was how the day started and ended. In a short period of time, Seth and Chelsea grew closer and shared intimate details of their lives. They conversed about their previous relationships and their children, as well as extended family. The topic arose as to how her family would disown her if they found out she was in a monogamous relationship with an African-American man. There was happiness and tears during their weekend together. They found something in each other that their former mates did not possess. In reality, it was the love of alcohol that controlled their feelings and emotions.

The weekend had come to an end and the ship was going back to sea the next day. Chelsea and Amy drove Seth and Dave back to the ship. Seth and Chelsea said their farewells and promised to keep in touch. Chelsea also responded with a flood of tears. Seth wondered if this was real or was it just something else Chelsea was going through. She had her many moments of crying, some of them real and others were a plea for attention. At that moment, Seth could not decipher the difference between the two. He was happy-go-lucky thinking he had found the woman of his dreams. The next day the ship left port. Seth and Chelsea kept in touch frequently by telephone and e-mail.

In October 1999, Chelsea purchased Seth a plane ticket for them to spend the weekend together. As Seth entered the terminal, he saw Chelsea at the bar finishing her drink. She ran up to him and gave him a hug and kiss. She was excited about the weekend they were going to spend together. After departing the airport, they went and got in Chelsea's car. Chelsea stated, "Have cooler—will travel." The cooler she had in the car had been packed with beer.

They arrived at the hotel and began spending their days and nights bar hopping. They did manage to find time for Chelsea to gamble at the casino. Of course, there were perks to it. They could drink free beer or mixed drinks while they were playing on the game tables or slot machines. Seth went back to the hotel room and Chelsea did not return until about an hour later. Then entered the arguments and excessively drinking alcohol. There was a pattern occurring that Seth did not recognize until later.

Despite the arguing, the two alcoholics were drunk and having fun together. The weekend came to a close and Seth flew back to where the ship located. The two of them continued calling and e-mailing. Chelsea did not work and had a lot of free time on her hand to drink.

In November 1999, Seth and Chelsea decided to meet for a weekend in Alabama so that he could meet her two children. Chelsea admitted that she did not have control over her children's bad manners.

After arriving in Alabama, Seth met Chelsea's two children and her Aunt. He also was introduced to her aunt's boyfriend. They were very pleasant people. Seth could tell Chelsea was at her whit's end with the way the boys were acting. She was right about their manners. They spent more time with X-Boxes, Play stations, drums, and computers (just to name a few). They hardly spent any time with their mother. She stated that she was embarrassed.

That evening Seth and Chelsea intimately conversed about other occurrences that took place in their lives. Seth explained his previous relationship leading to the present separation. Chelsea spoke of her battle with anorexia as a teenager. They later continued their conversation while walking through a nature park. The mood was right, so right that Seth proposed to Chelsea. With tears streaming down her cheeks as she said, "Yes!" In the back of Seth's mind, he pondered how her parents would react.

In December 1999, Seth flew once again to visit Chelsea. During his visit they went bowling together for the first time. Chelsea could bowl very well and Seth was average. During their bowling, Chelsea's mother called to ask what time would she be home so that her mother drop the dog off for dog sitting on New Year's evening. Chelsea gave her mother a time and she and Seth were back at Chelsea's house in time to dog sit. A strange thing happened when her mother dropped off the dog. She left the cage on the porch and blew the horn so Chelsea would come out and get the dog from the porch. Her mother had no desire to go inside and meet Chelsea's new fiancé. Well, that did not stop the fun. New Year's Eve was just like the rest of the visits, plenty of alcoholic beverages.

Seth visited Chelsea over the course of the next two months. As in good fashion, they spent most of their time in bars drinking alcohol.

During a February 2000 trip to Chelsea's house, her parents wanted to meet Seth during dinner. They finally met for the first time and all appeared to have gone well. However, within a few weeks Seth had to deploy for five months. Time on deployment seemed to be moving very slow. Seth was anxious to return to his fiancé. Although many times Seth had reservations about marrying Chelsea, he purchased her a bridal ring set.

The deployment came to an end and Seth transferred to Florida. He went on leave to marry his beloved Chelsea. She had located a house and now it was just a matter of tying the knot. The small, private July 2000 wedding took place in Tennessee. As Seth stood before his soon-to-be wife, his heart did not agree with what he was doing. He wrestled mentally by convincing himself that things will be fine and people change. The couple completed their vows and was now married.

The wedding night gave way to their first argument as husband and wife. Of course, it was attributed to the heavy drinking. The newlyweds had started their lives together. Now it was becoming evident that Chelsea's kids spent a lot of time by themselves playing computer and video games. Seth found out that being with someone who is bitter with others is unhealthy.

Seth was in and out of port frequently due to the demanding ship's schedule. His desire was to make a positive impact on her children's lives. The children seemed to respect Seth more than they did their own mother. While Seth was out to sea, Chelsea's parents were always there to assist in any way possible. They were wealthy people and showered Chelsea with money and a monthly credit card allowance. Seth benefited as well. One day when he had returned from a week out to sea, he was surprised to find a new truck waiting for him in the driveway. Chelsea's parents were generous in their giving. Seth felt that part of their giving was done to keep Chelsea and him happy and in their own little world. Seth helped Chelsea conceal her alcohol dependency from her parents.

In August 2000, Chelsea told Seth she was pregnant with their baby. She always wanted a baby girl and hoped her dreams would come true. Seth's mind went into overdrive. He wondered if she was going to stop drinking and smoking while pregnant. He further wondered what would happen while he was out to sea. Seth hoped that the pregnancy would bring about the changes needed to eliminate alcohol from the family.

Seth spent the next six of nine months out to sea. He found himself worrying day after day, more and more about Chelsea and the baby. Seth found refuge from worry by reading his Bible and praying everyday. He reflected on the times when he was a young boy attending church three to four times a week with his two sisters. Smiling, he remembers how some of his friends used to make fun of him. There were times when Seth harbored resentment while watching his friends play as he left to go to church.

Chelsea informed Seth that her mother was going to be with her during the last week of her pregnancy. In May 2001, Chelsea had a baby girl. This was three days before the ship returned. Seth received the message and was relieved to know that Chelsea and the baby were doing well. When the ship moored, Seth was one of the first to depart. It is a Navy tradition that new fathers depart the ship first to see their newborns. Seth found himself on the evening news as reporters were on the pier covering the return of the ship. Seth was able to hold his baby girl for the first time. However, the first thing Chelsea offered Seth as they were secured in the car was a beer. He wondered if she had been drinking during her pregnancy. Seth's first evening home was full of drinks and an empty feeling inside.

Seth received information that he had been selected for a U.S. Navy commission. Once he accepted the commission, the family would have to move to Washington State. Seth had always wanted to go out west because he is an avid hunter and that would provide him an opportunity to experience hunting there. Chelsea was excited about going. Chelsea's two boys took it the hardest because they thought it would be hard for them to make new friends. Seth was sure they would find friends because they had every video game and game system on the market. They had everything a child could ask for—except love.

The only time the two boys would be seen is when they came out of their room to eat. The only time they seemed happy is when they knew they were going to visit their father. The boys expressed numerous times that they wanted to live with their father because their mother drank too much and at times they were embarrassed to have friends come over.

One day, Seth had the opportunity to converse with Chelsea's ex-husband without her monitoring their conversation. Seth was surprised to find that Chelsea had been in a rehabilitation facility on two occasions during her first marriage. He wondered why she had not mentioned this to him. He thought that this may be the reason she could not keep a job. Seth thought she only had a drinking problem and could stop when she wanted to. Chelsea was an alcoholic and the only way she could stop drinking was if she received professional help and a change of lifestyle.

In May 2002, Seth and Chelsea travelled to Washington State to start a new beginning. Already in their first two years of marriage, there were times when alcohol almost destroyed their family and as well as the marriage itself. While travelling, the scenery was beautiful. However when they made stops for the evenings, drinks were included everywhere they went. Seth was no different than Chelsea. There were times when arguments would occur because Seth did not desire more to drink. Although she still poured him one, Seth would eventually drink it. In private, Seth prayed that things would change in his life.

They arrived safely at their new home in Washington State. They purchased a beautiful home overlooking a year round, snow-top mountain. The children arrived with their grandmother by airplane a few days later.

Seth was now a Naval Officer and was very pleased with his new job and new friends he had met. When the ship left port to go out to sea, Seth was concerned about Chelsea. She had recently found a casino not too far from their home. As long as she gambled, the drinks were free.

Surprisingly, Chelsea managed to find herself a job. Seth felt better knowing she would be working and not at home drinking alcohol. Yet, Chelsea went to work with the smell of alcohol on her breath. To make matters worse, there was a liquor store in the vicinity of her place of work. Seth confronted her about alcohol at work, however she denied it.

There were incidents where the police had to be called to the Pearson household due to Chelsea's alcohol abuse. Chelsea was also obsessed with bowling. She felt that she was not a good bowler unless she was drinking. The routine was simple, the casino and bowling or visiting friends. Seth had fallen into denial of everything that was going on.

Once, Seth returned from a deployment and Chelsea had booked a cruise for them. The cruise was a disaster. Seth wondered if Chelsea remembered any of it, since she remained drunk the entire time.

The next two years that followed were equally as challenging. Chelsea stated many times that she wanted Seth to leave but when she was sober, things went back to normal, whatever normal is. There were several times when Seth wanted to give up. From drinking to arguing, then enters multiple personalities, all to which had taken its toll on Seth.

In February 2004, Seth and his family were returning east coast. Seth was happy to leave bad memories behind. The trip was like déjà vu. Constant drinking was the standard and if it was altered in anyway, that created a problem.

The arguments occurred more frequently and the drinking seemed to be the way to live. Seth was able to uphold his image as a Naval Officer but deep down inside there was pain and unhappiness. He had reached the point where he did not desire to go home. His daughter was his reason for not giving up.

In May 2004, Chelsea asked Seth to come home from work because she was not feeling well. Seth came home to find Chelsea in bed. He looked into her eyes and saw a darkness he had never seen before. Soon after, she had a seizure. Seth told Chelsea's youngest son to dial 9-1-1. The look of fear consumed his face. With two fire trucks, police car, and ambulance on the scene, Seth had reached his limit.

Neighbors were gathered outside wondering what had happened. Seth distraughtly followed the ambulance to the hospital. The doctor said that Chelsea had experienced an alcohol withdrawal seizure and could have died if she were there alone. To safely "detox" Chelsea required her to stay in the hospital for a few days in the Intensive Care Unit (ICU). Chelsea signed herself out of the ICU and there was nothing anyone could do.

Seth drove Chelsea home. Being heavily medicated, she did not know who he was or where she lived. Seth was hurt by this entire ordeal and was afraid to allow the children to see their mother this way.

Taking matter into his hands, Seth called and requested a court order to get her back into the hospital. Within a few hours, the court order was approved and the police went to take Chelsea into custody. It was another embarrassing moment, with five police cars in front of his house and his wife being escorted in handcuffs. Now, all those within the vicinity of our home knew she was an alcoholic. There was no more hiding the fact.

Chelsea made it through *detox* but refused going to be rehabilitated. Seth could take no more, he cried out loudly for help from God. Seth began to draw closer to God. He renewed his life and asked the Lord and Savior, Jesus Christ, to come in and have His way. He began attending church again. This time he took the rest of the family with him.

Meantime, Chelsea started back drinking within a few days of her hospital release. She stated that she would (and she did) attend church on her own accord. He overlooked the fact that she smelled of alcohol when she returned home. She eventually turned herself in to a treatment facility three times in two years. Seth found out she was having an affair. Seth, now allowing God to piece his life back together realized he could not change her.

In January 2005, Chelsea hit bottom again and decided to admit herself in a rehabilitation facility. Seth made the arrangements and her father paid $15,000 for her stay. During her stay, Chelsea's two boys decided they could no longer take living with their mother and demanded to live with their father. Arrangements were made and the boys went to live with their father. Their father soon thereafter received custody of them.

Upon completion of rehabilitation, Chelsea made a strong impression that she wanted to stay sober. Seth agreed to Chelsea having custody of their daughter if she agreed to stay sober during their divorce proceedings. Chelsea now lives with their daughter and her new husband whom she met in the rehabilitation facility.

Seth depended on God and is a born again Christian. He understands that the Bible expressly teaches us that sin (drunkenness) is overcome by faith in Christ, "He is made unto us wisdom, righteousness, sanctification, and redemption." "He is the way, the truth, and the life." Christians are said to "purify their hearts by faith" (Acts 15:9). In Acts 26:18 it is affirmed that the Christians are sanctified by faith in Christ.

2

ALCOHOLIC SELECTION

What do I personally know about alcohol and its abuses? Everything a man can know and survive. The man depicted in the story is me. I am "Seth."

I know that just as people differ in every other peculiarity, so they differ—and differ greatly—in their capacity for enjoying indulgence in alcohol. Some are satisfied with very moderate indulgence; others crave for the deepest intoxication. Between the extremes lie all shades of drinkers. It is plain, also, that, as a rule, people drink in proportion to their desires. We see that alcohol is a poison. It is only reasonable to conclude that alcohol poisons to the greatest extent those who drink more of it.

It is true that some people are able to tolerate much greater quantities of alcohol than others. Nevertheless, even those whose tolerance is the greatest are more injured by a large quantity. Year after year, alcohol eliminates a great number of people since alcohol weeds out enormous numbers of people of a particular type, it is a stringent agent of selection—an agent of selection more stringent than any one disease. Many diseases have been the cause of great and manifest change. It follows that alcohol should be the cause of change at least as great as that which has been caused by any other disease.

The public, supported by the great majority of the medical profession, suppose that the effects produced by alcohol on parents are transmitted to offspring. The language used by some writers seems to imply even a belief that parental drunkenness causes an actual longing for the substance alcohol in the child.

I strongly believe that every drunkard's desire for alcohol must contain three necessary factors, one inborn and two acquired. First, the drunkard must be so constituted as to be capable of enjoying deep indulgence. Therefore, no one would be drunken who was not capable of enjoying drink—whether as a means of deriving positive pleasure, or as a means of relieving physical and mental discomfort or pain. This factor is certainly inborn, and therefore as certainly transmissible to offspring. The person having it is cursed with the "alcohol diathesis," with the "predisposition" to drunkenness. Most people are keenly capable of enjoying drink, and their offspring inherit the capacity.

The second factor is the drunkard's knowledge of alcohol—his or her actual recollection of the pleasurable sensations which aroused former acts of drunkenness. Without this second factor (this actual experience of drink), no one can crave for alcohol in the sense meant. People who have never tasted alcohol, may desire it as a thing of which they have only heard about. They cannot crave for it with that kind of craving, which the drunkard feels. No one will maintain that a child inherits its parent's recollections. Therefore it is plain that the actual craving for drink is never transmitted. In the absence of actual personal experience of alcohol, there can be no desire (in the sense meant) for it. It is scarcely necessary to continue this point of view.

Besides the capacity for enjoying alcohol, and the actual recollections of the sensations evoked by alcohol, every drunkard's desire contains a third factor. The more a drinker indulges in drink, the more within limits does he or she crave for it. I say within limits, because the growth of the craving does not continue indefinitely. After a time it ceases to increase. However, the limits vary widely with different individuals. The increase is small in the typically moderate man; yet, it is great in the typical inebriate. Therefore, the craving does not develop at once; it grows with indulgence. It is true some people are so constituted that the very first experience of drink appears to awaken in them a furious desire for deep indulgence. It is probable that, even in them, the appetite grows with feeding. At any rate, it is certainly true that it grows in most drunkards. It is this growth of craving that some writers generally allude to when they say the craving for drink is transmitted. They suppose that a man or woman's drinking increases his or her capacity for enjoying and craving for alcohol. They think that this increase of appetite is transmitted to offspring.

Some writers have founded their belief on the indisputable fact that drunkenness tends to run in families. In other words, on the fact that drunken parents tend to have children who in turn are drunken. Here we come to a very fine, but vastly important point. A drunkard drinks because he or she is so constituted, that experience of alcohol awakens in him a craving for alcohol. Whether they drink or not, they tend to transmit this inborn constitution of mind to their child(ren). Many individuals whose parents and ancestors never tasted alcohol become exceedingly drunk when given the opportunity. Their parents had the capacity for enjoying drink, but had not opportunity of indulging it. Again, people who, against their natural inclination, are abstainers (from moral and prudential motives), often have drunken children. The fact that drunkenness tends to run in families, therefore, does not of itself constitute a proof that parental drinking is a cause of filial intemperance. It is merely an instance of the universally admitted truth that children tend to inherit the inborn characters of the parent. Big parents tend to have big children; fair parents, fair children; parents so constituted as to find delight in alcohol tend to have children similarly constituted.

Even if it were true that parental drinking increased the child's tendency to drink, we could not, by observing the drunken children of drunken parents, find proof. We could not, by observation, separate the portion of the child's tendency (which was due to mere inheritance of the parent's inborn capacity for enjoying drink) from the increase of tendency which resulted from the parent's drinking. The voluminous statistics that the medical profession and others have compiled, and which prove that drunken parents tend to have drunken children, have, therefore, no bearing on the point at issue. It would be as reasonable to suppose, because a man enjoys and eats peaches and grapes, and has a son who also enjoys peaches and grapes that the child's enjoyment of these edibles is due to the father's indulgence in them. Clearly the proposition is absurd. The child's inborn likes and dislikes depend on something deeper than the mere acquirements of the parent. Individuals, whose parents and ancestors had no previous experience of peaches or grapes, enjoy them quite as much as other people. The case of alcohol is precisely similar. It is just as absurd to suppose that, because a drunken parent has a drunken child, that the parent's drinking is the cause of the child's predisposition to drink.

Again, some writers have published statistics, or mere statements, declaring that they have observed "degeneracy" in the children of drunkards. They suppose further that "degeneracy," predisposes offspring to intemperance. However, no evidence is forthcoming that it does predispose to intemperance, and degeneracy may be observed in the children of non-drunkards. So numerous are the sources of error that it is not possible to obviate the confusion, except by statistics on an enormous scale. They would have to be compiled with the most exact care by those trained to the closest habits of scientific observation, totally free from all prejudice, and possessed of a full knowledge of the conditions of the problem. Most statistics published do not fulfill these requirements.

We must turn for enlightenment to another line of reasoning. A character acquired by the parent, if transmitted, would appear as an inborn character in the child. Now, to take an illustration we have already used, if a father were blinded by accident, and his child, as a consequence, were born blind, the father's blindness would be acquired, but the child's would be inborn. Inborn traits, as we know, are transmissible to future generations. The increased capacity for enjoying alcohol which indulgence confers is an acquirement. If transmitted, it would appear in the offspring as an inborn trait, and would tend, as a consequence, to be inherited by succeeding generations also. In other words, not only would the son be affected by the drinking of the parent, but future generations as well. It is plain, on this hypothesis (i.e. that parental drinking increases the child's predisposition to drunkenness), that the effects of drinking would accumulate generation after generation—each succeeding generation being rendered more and more inclined to drunkenness by the drinking of preceding generations. The son would inherit his father's capacity for delighting in alcohol, plus the increment caused by the father's drinking. He would make a different start in life, in that he would begin with a greater proneness to drunkenness than the father began with. The grandson would start with the son's initial proneness, plus the increment caused by the son's drinking. This process, repeated for many generations, would evidently render the race so very inclined to drink, and, as a consequence, so very drunken, that, given the opportunity, it would drink to extinction.

I understate the case however. For the son, owing to his greater capacity for enjoying alcohol, would, as a rule, drink more than the father, and therefore transmit a greater increment of the predisposition to drunkenness to the grandson than the father transmitted to him. The same would happen in succeeding generations. The proneness to drink would increase in a sort of geometrical progression. The race would rush to ruin. In a very few generations it would become extinct. Exactly the same would happen did parental alcoholism produce filial degeneration.

On the other hand, if parental drinking does not increase the child's proneness to drunkenness, the result must be quite different. Alcoholic selection is very stringent. The children of drunkards, inherit (as a rule) the parental character, and tend to be eliminated by drink, are generally placed under conditions much less favorable than those which surround the offspring of more temperate individuals. At worst, they are neglected, ill-nourished and live in poorer and unsanitary homes. Not all, but most. As a consequence, they perish in greater numbers. Very frequently the worst alcoholics—those who have quickly and violently developed the craving for intoxication—do not marry. Indulgence ruins their appearance, and renders them mentally and physically unattractive to the opposite sex. Men and women object to ally themselves to known inebriates. Male drunkards are very apt to satisfy their sexual cravings by intercourse with an unfortunate and very sterile class of women, who are often unfortunate because drunken. Deaths indirectly attributable to alcohol swell the total of those directly attributable to it. To their sum must be added all those offspring which drunkards might have, but do not have.

Here, then, is a method by which we may discover the effect that parental drinking has on offspring. If we find that people grow increasingly degenerate (or prone to intemperance) the longer they use alcohol, then we may accept as proved the doctrine that parental drinking is through heredity a cause of offspring deterioration or insobriety. On the other hand, if we find that people grow increasingly sober under the influence of alcohol, we must accept as proved the contrary assumption. In that case the most voluminous of statistics ought not to alter our decision. Such statistics do not at present exist. Only a popular superstition and a few vague and ill-digested guesses exist.

3

THE CAUSES OF
DRUNKENNESS

Knowing first hand the causes of drunkenness, drinkers of alcohol may be divided roughly into three classes. In the first class, many people drink merely to satisfy thirst. They take alcohol, and the other special constituents of intoxicating beverages, as they might take lemon-juice, simply to make the water they drink more tasteful. They drink for the same reason as they eat—a necessary constituent of their bodies has become deficient, and they seek to supply it. They add alcohol to their water as they add sauces to their meat. They take the alcohol as they take the sauce, not for the sake of the flavoring agent, but for the sake of the thing it flavors. Such people, when actuated by thirst alone, are never drunkards. They prefer the more dilute solutions of alcohol, usually light wines and beers, which contain in greatest abundance the particular constituent they desire—water. Having had enough of the water, they take no more of the flavoring agent—alcohol. In the absence of wine or beer, they can be satisfied with water otherwise flavored, as with tea or coffee.

In the second class, they drink intoxicating beverages, not so much from thirst, as for the sake of the flavoring agents. They delight in the

taste of some solutions of alcohol. They drink, as a person eats chocolate, to produce a delightful sensation in the mouth. They are generally connoisseurs and drinkers of wines. Very few of them drink beer
or liquor, except perhaps to excite the desire. The taste of beer and
spirits is not sufficiently delightful. The true connoisseurs are wine-
drinkers. Bad wine disgusts them. Of good wine they prolong their
enjoyment as long as possible, holding it to the light, smelling it, sip-
ping it, rolling it in their mouth and round their palates. In every way,
they get as much of its beauty, aroma, and taste as they can. Such
drinkers are rarely drunkards. Small amounts disgust them, just as the
average person is disgusted by a moderate amount of chocolate. To
them the first glass is the most enjoyable; but, as they drink, their
sense of taste become hindered, and at length the finest wines no
longer give pleasure through the sense of taste.

The third class of drinkers, drink not for the satisfaction of thirst, nor
for the gratification of the sense of taste, but to produce that mental
effect which we call drunkenness. Individuals who call for a quart of
beer, and, after gulping it down, departs satisfied, desires a pleasure
evidently quite different from that which moves connoisseurs, toying
with their rare wines. Both, again, desire gratifications totally different in kind from which drunkards seek when they indulge to excess.

People therefore drink alcoholic beverages, first, to satisfy thirst, an
organic craving for a necessary constituent of the body—water; second, to gratify the sense of taste, or produce a sensation of pleasure
through excitation of the peripheral nerve endings in the mouth; and
third, to produce a stimulation (or what feels like a stimulation), but
which soon becomes a daze or partial paralysis. Though people drink
for three separate reasons, it must not be supposed that all drinkers are
sharply separable into three distinct categories. The same person, at
the same time, may drink to satisfy his or her thirst, palate, and craving for drunkenness.

At first, drinks may desire to satisfy their thirst, next to gratify theirs sense of taste, and lastly they may seek for intoxication. Yet, at the beginning of their drinking career, they may drink primarily to satisfy their thirst or taste, and, at the end, primarily to gratify a craving for intoxication. However, the fact remains, that, while many people drink merely to satisfy thirst or taste, the principal motives with others is to obtain those feelings of intoxication which alcohol produces when acting, directly on the central nervous system. It has been necessary to draw these distinctions clearly, because much confusion exists in the public mind. The extreme wing of the temperance party regards all drinkers as drunkards, who differ only in degree. A drunkard is often spoken of as a thirsty soul. Moderate drinkers (those who drink merely to satisfy thirst or taste) are never real drunkards. Real drunkards are not thirsty souls. They drink, not because they are thirsty, but because they crave for that mental state, or paresis, which we call drunkenness.

It may be argued that, since pure alcohol (diluted with water) cannot gratify drinkers' palate, and since the smallest amount of alcohol circulating in the blood must produce some effect on the brain, everyone who drinks alcohol is to some extent a drunkard. You see, the argument is easy to understand. Something unpleasant in itself may be pleasant as a flavoring agent (i.e. cayenne pepper). Moreover, drunkards are those who drink alcohol until they are mentally weakened to a degree more or less perceptible. It is with these mentally weakened people that we have to deal. Without them, the temperance problem would not exist, in spite of thirsty souls and connoisseurs. In the future, when I speak of the effects produced by alcohol, I am not alluding to thirst or taste, but solely to the direct effect of alcohol on the brain—to its effects as an intoxicant.

Not only do people differ in regards to their motives for drinking alcohol, but those who use alcohol as an intoxicant differ immensely in degree also. The full and clear recognition of this fact is so important that it is necessary to dwell on it at length. People differ in all their mental and physical parts, in size, strength, shape, color, their mathematical, artistic, and other faculties, in their capacity for enjoying tobacco, salt, or sugar. There is no single character in which people do not differ in degree. Judging by analogy, it is certain that they are not equal in their enjoyment of alcohol. To put it more precisely, in the amount of alcohol they are capable of finding enjoyable. Just as some people are satisfied with a single pipe of tobacco, so some are satisfied with the effect produced by a single glass of alcohol at meal times, or as a "nightcap" before retiring to bed. Others desire deeper indulgence; they are not satisfied until distinctly appreciable mental ill-effects are produced. Yet, others desire complete intoxication.

Now it is only reasonable to say that, as a rule, people drink in proportion to their desires. Therefore, the deep drinker (generally speaking) is one so constituted mentally that deep indulgence is delightful to him. However, the moderate drinker is one to whom moderate indulgence is more pleasant. For illustration; suppose two women are equal in regards to moral training, willpower, opportunities of procuring alcohol, and everything else, except their delight in alcohol. It is only reasonable to expect that she who has the stronger desire will be the more likely to yield to temptation. So, women indulge in sugar, salt, tobacco, or anything else in proportion to their desires. Of course, there are exceptions to this rule. Human life is very complex; alcohol is not the only factor that determines our actions.

I speak only of the general rule. I suppose the people who are so constituted as to be much tempted by alcohol, yields more often, than those who are so constituted as to be less tempted. The contrary assumption involves the obvious absurdity that all people are equal in their delight in (and, therefore, desire for) alcohol.

It does not enter the mind that people may be temperate, and yet exercise no self-control. They may be sober because deep indulgence is not agreeable to them. Self-control is not alleged to be a principal factor in abstinence from, or moderation in, the use of tobacco. It is manifest that most smokers indulge to near the limit of their capacity for enjoyment. However, deep drinking does much harm, and therefore self-control is urged. Because it is urged, the mistake is made of supposing that it is the only (or the principal) factor in the causation of sobriety. As a fact, self-control is the principal factor only in those exceptional cases in which the moderate drinker, or abstainer, has both the craving for drunkenness and the opportunity of gratifying it.

Now ask yourself, are you an abstainer or a drunkard? Like most people of the better classes, you may be neither and call yourself a moderate drinker. Are you, then, temperate only because you exercise self-control? Is your answer "Yes?" If so, from the bottom of my heart, I have sympathy for you. Continually tormented by your unsatisfied craving for drunkenness, you must be a miserable being—a being only one degree less miserable than an actual drunkard. I, most certainly, have been where you are. I recall times in my life where I had to live with someone who resisted the craving for alcohol. However, I am temperate, not because I have resisted temptation, but through a fortunate lack of it. I do not have what doctors call the alcohol diathesis. As I tour the states training and sharing a message of living an abundant life to those who are alcoholics, I have found that most of the people that I met were temperate manifestly without effort. A little alcohol satisfied them, more had awakened sensations which, on the whole, were unpleasant. Yes, a certain group of moderate drinkers—who generally drink somewhat more—had doubtless enjoyed deeper indulgence, but the craving was not so strong as to balance their dislike to the consequences. Now, the remainder, were so driven to alcohol that, ignoring the remote consequences, they sought immediate satisfaction and were intemperate.

I am sure, in spite of drinkers' hasty declaration of a proneness to drunkenness, that their personal experience, supposing them to be an average member of better-class society, is similar. Let them also think of those with whom they are brought into social contact, particularly of those with whom they are most intimate, their own relatives. Have they observed in their wives or mothers, for instance, a tendency to intemperance, checked only by a sense of duty? Are their fathers, brothers, and sisters victims of this miserable craving, as they are "victims" of the cravings for food and water? I think if they and their relatives are average people, they will recognize, on reflection, that they are temperate, not in spite of their inclinations, but because of them. In fact, alcohol does not tempt them to drunkenness, but to a mild indulgence only. They must know people in their own class of life so differently constituted that alcohol does tempt them to intoxication, notwithstanding that they have had the same advantages of education and environment that he or she has had. Deep indulgence affords them keen pleasure, or of mental pain.

It is often argued, since no one begins life with a craving for alcohol, and since a more or less prolonged indulgence is usually necessary before anyone acquires the drunkard's craving, that drunkards are of worse upbringing, or of weaker wills, than others. In other words, some people think that the moderate person is temperate merely because, through training or choice, he or she exercises self-control early and always. They also think that the deep drinkers are drunk because they never exercise self-control. This view is in error because all the factors are not taken into account. Everyone starts life without any craving for alcohol. They differ largely with respect to the ease in which the craving may be awakened and the strength it may attain.

Moreover, the assumption that temperate individuals are necessarily strong-minded, whereas drunken men are necessarily weak-minded, has no foundation in fact. History and everyday experience abound with instances to the contrary. It is a simple truth that the will of mankind is exercised to gratify our desires. People of powerful will who has an ardent craving for drink are generally drunk. They use their powers to gratify their strong desire. The weak individual will often use his or her opportunity; the strong individual will generally make it.

4

THE CAUSES OF
ALCOHOLISM

All the terrible things resulting from the use of alcohol: poverty, misery, insanity, crime, waste of time, money, food, land and human life are grouped together under the name Alcoholism. I feel this is one of the greatest afflictions of mankind, affecting (as I have seen) the individual, family and State. I am commonly asked, "Why do people drink alcohol since it produces bad results?" It is necessary that I answer this question in writing so that others may understand what remedy (or remedies) may be applied.

When a doctor is called to see a sick person, he endeavors to find out what is the cause of the illness. Until this is found and removed, the patient cannot be completely cured. Alcoholism is a social disease of which the causes are many. Therefore, it is necessary to investigate carefully what these causes are in order to know how to remove them, or at least to deal with them in such a way as to diminish their power.

I have learned through my own experience that the first and most important cause of alcoholism is ignorance of the real nature of alcohol and its effects on the body. I am surprised at some of the beliefs of many people I speak with. Some people believe that it is useful and beneficial, that it nourishes and strengthens the body, and produces energy for work. Some believe that it assists them to bear fatigue, to resist exposure and to endure the cold weather. Others believe that it dispels sickness, relieves hunger and soothes the stomach. All these beliefs are false. Alcohol does none of these things. If its claims are examined, in every case it does the exact opposite. Why do people believe the opposite of the truth? The answer lies in the action of alcohol on the brain. It is essentially a deceiver; it deadens and paralyses the highest parts of the brain so that a anyone under its influence is no longer a competent judge of his or her thoughts, feelings or actions.

A second group of causes is found in the instinct of imitation, the force of habit, and the tyranny of social habits and customs. Many drink in order to do as others do, even when they have no wish to drink, and when there is no need to satisfy thirst. They model their conduct on the example of those around them and have no willpower of their own. They drink merely because their companions drink. This is especially dangerous to young people who are in High School and who have begun to start life's work. Freed from the discipline to which they have been accustomed (and allowed to spend the greater part of the earned money as they please) they are apt to imitate the foolishness of others and so fall into evil habits. They should exercise special care in this period of their lives, to develop the character that they may be able to think and act wisely and prudently for themselves and not merely be the imitators of others.

A third important cause of alcoholism is the abundance, variety and cheapness of alcoholic liquors. Alcohol is now produced from a great number of substances. All the resources of science have been called in to assist in its production and millions of dollars are expended in its manufacture and distribution.

A fourth cause of alcoholism is found in the conditions under which so many people live and work. The hard worker, the doctor exhausted from the long hours of the day, the construction person who has for hours been standing in the blazing sun, those firefighters day is spent amid dreary and depressing surroundings; all the thousands of military men and women often deployed for long periods away from family; several of these have stated that they turn to alcohol for relief. However, alcohol only serves to increase their exhaustion.

Another cause of alcoholism is the influence of heredity. Alcohol not only injures drinkers but it injures their children. They have greater difficulty in resisting the temptation to drink than the children of sober parents. Alcohol does not produce its terrible effects in one generation only, but introduces the characteristics and behaviors to the next.

Lastly, we have selfishness, sensuality and wickedness as causes of alcoholism. There are several wealthy people who are not fatigued by any daily task are often victims of this social disease. They explained that it is not misery, discomfort of body, or mind that causes them to run to alcohol. They want something to gratify their appetites and procure pleasure of a sensual kind. They live on a lower level and allow uncontrolled passions to rule over their intellectual and spiritual being.

The causes of alcoholism are numerous, and in order to destroy or diminish this social plague we must, as a start, be prepared understand the reasons to stop drinking alcohol. As we know, the effects of alcohol are physical, mental, and moral. Attention is here directed to the moral effect upon the drinker.

5

TEN REASONS TO STOP DRINKING ALCOHOL

There are certain well-pronounced results following indulgence in alcohol which manifest themselves in the moral nature of the person, and among them:

1. *Drinking alcohol stupefies the intellect.* The brain is the organ of the mind and the center of personality. Alcohol seeks the brain, for which it seems to have an especial affinity. Quite a large portion of the alcohol taken into the system is carried by the circulation into the brain. There it works its havoc and does its paralyzing hurt on the most important and delicate organ of the human anatomy. When this special organ is assailed by alcohol, one's moral energies instantly become obscure or utterly vanish. This is the first, most direct and pronounced effect of alcohol on the human system. It exhibits itself immediately in the inability of its victims to control their appetite or to limit their indulgence. This leaves the flood-gate wide open, while the keeper is away—immorality and excess run riot. The brain is paralyzed, and nothing stops its mad rush to destruction. They have literally put an enemy into their stomach to steal away their brain. "The pilot is dead; the ship is driven before the fury of the storm to the rocks."

2. *Drinking alcohol weakens moral resistance.* It silences the voice of conscience. By stupefying the intellect, it obliterates the moral sense accordingly. Right and wrong no longer represent moral obligations, even moral distinctions. This is the cause of the crimes that crowd the calendars of the courts and the columns of the daily newspapers. So dehumanized are those under the influence of alcohol that there is a constant tendency to extenuate crimes committed. They say, "It was not me, but the alcohol, that did it." True, alcohol was a driving factor but its poor victim knew it would, and therefore cannot be exonerated. The moral sense of mankind cannot be persuaded by such deceptive pleading. The man who enters a house and commits theft is a criminal, but so is the neighbor who furnished the key to enter.

3. *Drinking alcohol impairs sensibility.* It destroys the affections of the heart. The victims lose their love for their friends, wives, husbands, children, or parents. All bonds of love are broken and all ties of affection are severed in the moral wreck of alcohol. Not only love of home and friends, but all love for property, industry, economy, and self-respect, the wish to better one's condition and the desire for people's good will are all remorselessly swept away. Herein lies the tragedy of the home and the marriage relation. This is what crowds the divorce courts with destroyed human happiness. One heart dies, another breaks. Drinking alcohol destroys love. A major newspaper reported that nearly one hundred divorces were granted in four courts in one day. The judges said that alcohol was the cause of nearly every one of them.

4. *Drinking alcohol paralyzes the will.* It touches all faculties of the soul, clouds the intellect, and hardens the heart. It weakens and binds the will, and makes it impossible for the trapped victim to be independent, to rise up in moral freedom, or to fight against its invader. The drinkers' moral resistance goes down before the attack of alcohol. This condition can mean nothing less than excess, indulgence, crime, or

helpless misery. Immorality or idiocy cannot be a matter of surprise, but it can be an indispensable necessity of brain-poisoning by alcohol.

5. *Drinking alcohol creates hallucinations.* It makes drinkers think that they are rich, imagine that they are smart that their company is desirable, that they are capable of doing almost any impossible thing, and that they can stop drinking whenever they want to though they never want to. They easily persuade themselves that with liquor they can do more and better work than without it. Drinkers are often sure that they are being cured of sickness by alcohol, so of course they take it "as a medicine." They absolutely know that they have some disorder that nothing but alcohol will overcome. They also know that it is necessary for their health and without it they could not perform their tasks. The poor, self-deceived alcoholics drink themselves into the grave and die "cured." In all these respects the alcohol fiend is self-deluded. The facts are that they do less work and of a poorer quality with alcohol than without it. They are worse, physically and are not being cured but killed. It truly comes to pass that "Wine *is* a mocker, Strong drink *is* a brawler, And whoever is led astray by it is not wise." (Proverbs 20:1)

6. *Drinking alcohol produces cravings for more alcohol.* No harmless beverage or wholesome food ever produces the effect of demand for more as Alcoholic beverages does. They disturb the order of nature and create abnormal conditions. Herein is the main source of their deadly harm. What an infinite curse God would have put on humanity if the use of food always fired up the passion for more, and created a craving for excess. Yet, wholesome food or drink taken into the system stops the craving and satisfies the appetite. It safeguards the life instead of destroying it. Alcohol reverses all this. Drinkers who seek to drown their trouble in alcohol are immediately submerged by an ocean of greater troubles. They are like the people who, finding their homes empty and garnished, "Then he goes and takes with *him* seven other spirits more wicked than himself, and they enter and dwell there; and

the last *state* of that man is worse than the first." (Luke 11:26, Matthew 12:45)

7. *Drinking alcohol creates unrest and dissatisfaction.* Life becomes weary, stale, flat, unprofitable, and disgusting. The victims of alcohol cannot get themselves interested in anything. Work wearies them. Books and study do not appeal to them. They cannot concentrate their thoughts. They cannot employ their mental powers on any subject that requires intellectual activity. Life loses color, taste, hope, and energy. One thing only seems worthwhile—alcohol. One thought only inspires their imagination—alcohol. One supreme passion only consumes them—alcohol. Everything else is profitless, meaningless, undesirable, and unbearable. No moral appeal reaches them. Closed to all moral incentives, they are open to the attacks of corruption and easily become the agents of crime. They have ceased to value their own life, why should they place a high estimate on the lives of others, even that of their spouses or children? Life has lost its zest for them, why should they have terror for thought of life in a penitentiary? A palace or a prison, a temple or a grave are all the same to those who have burnt out life's incense.

8. *Drinking alcohol weakens honesty and honor.* It generally destroys them both. Alcoholics will lie, cheat, deceive, and dissemble anything in order to get more alcohol for continuance of their ruin. Children, otherwise honest, will deceive their parents. Spouses will deceive one another to obtain alcohol, or to induce them to believe that they have not been drinking. There is almost nothing in the way of lying and deception that alcoholics will not do. Their moral natures are impaired, if not wrecked, and all sense of honor is correspondingly dismantled. What a sacrifice made (for an hour of pleasure) to allow such a harmful agent into their systems to destroy their lives.

9. *Drinking alcohol drowns self-respect and destroys adulthood.* When we see the finished product of alcohol—the thin, emaciated form, trembling hand, bleared or bloodshot eye, ragged clothes, and staggering

walk, we do not need to ask for the cause. Alcohol has destroyed a life and wrecked a soul. When we see the alcoholic sleeping in dry goods boxes or under the highway over-paths, cleaning soda cans to drink out of and cringingly begging for money to obtain liquor, we do not have to be told that adulthood and honor have gone down into a bottomless pit never to rise again. That poor, lost soul can be easily made the tool of wickedness and the agent of crime. Most, dare not seek for honest living or for honorable employment.

10. *Drinking alcohol destroys the spiritual life.* All moral motives that have their inspiration and support in religion weaken, dissolve, and vanish. Neither the love of God, fear of Hell, nor the hope of Heaven make any appeal to the soul or exert any influence on the conduct. Sadly, alcoholics no longer believe in God, nor do they ask for His help. All invitations based on religion, immortality, Heaven, Hell, eternity, and God fall on deaf ears and unresponsive hearts. One cup of alcohol outweighs them all. Therefore, we do not wonder that when our spiritual nature is dead and all our religious hopes have perished, we are at the mercy of every suggestion of wickedness and every temptation of crime. Such a state furnishes the fatal condition for the perpetration of wicked acts. Immorality is its very breath. Wickedness is the magnolia blossom of such planting.

I was one of the millions of alcoholics, and of the thousands who pass into the picture of despair. Is the spirit of alcohol more potent than the Spirit of God?

Just as I have, you may go free if you choose. Yes, there is Divine mercy for us all. You may become the victor over alcohol if you so desire. The crushed soul may be healed. The broken heart may be bound up. The inflamed appetite may be cooled. The wrecked nerves may be reinvigorated. The Great Physician is not unwilling to undertake nor unable to cure all who come to Him by faith.

"Let the wicked forsake his way, And the unrighteous man his thoughts; Let him return to the LORD, And He will have mercy on him; And to our God, For He will abundantly pardon." (Isaiah 55:7)

"Therefore He is also able to save to the uttermost those who come to God through Him, since He always lives to make intercession for them." (Hebrews 7:25)

Those that go to Him will in no way be rejected. Alcoholic's cases are desperate, but they need not despair. They must ask with all their heart for the help of Jesus Christ, who tasted death for mankind. The Bible says for everyone that thirsts come to the waters and to buy the wine and milk of the gospel without money and without price. God, who made the body, certainly knows how to repair it when we destroy it with alcohol. He created and redeemed the soul and knows how to cleanse it from all sin and to present it faultless before His throne.

Therefore, let no drinker, drunkard, or alcoholic despair. You can be saved if you want to; and you will be saved if you ask to. Accept Jesus Christ as the Savior from sin, alcohol, appetite, and Hell, and you will live. Do not fear. I invite you, for He has said that if we come to Him that He will not cast us out!

6

OBTAINING GUIDANCE FROM GOD

(SEVEN STEPS)

We come now face to face with the question of how to obtain guidance from God. There are seven steps, clearly set forth in the Word of God, in the path that leads to God's guidance.

The *first step* toward obtaining God's guidance is that we accept the Lord Jesus Christ as our own personal Savior, and surrender to Him as our Lord and Master. This comes out very plainly in James 1:5, "If any of you lacks wisdom, let him ask of God, who gives to all liberally and without reproach, and it will be given to him." It is clear that the promise is only made to believers. James does **not** say, "If any *man* lacks wisdom, let him ask of God." He said, "If any *of you* lacks wisdom, let him ask of God." There is no promise in the Word of God that God will guide anyone but the believer in Jesus Christ. Indeed there is no promise in the Word of God that He will answer the prayers of unbelievers about anything. God's guidance is the privilege of the believer in Jesus Christ and of Him alone. By believer I do not mean the one who merely has an orthodox faith about Jesus Christ, but the one who is a believer in the Bible sense, that is, the one who has that living faith in Jesus Christ that leads him to receive Jesus Christ as his Lord and Savior, and to surrender his life to His service and control. If then, we would have God's sure guidance, the first thing to make sure of is that we really are believers, that we really are children of God, that we really have accepted Jesus Christ as our Savior, and really have surrendered our lives to His Lordship.

The *second step* toward obtaining God's guidance is that we clearly realize our own inability to decide for ourselves the way in which we should go. The promise, as we find it in the Word of God, makes this very plain. James says, "If any of you lacks wisdom, let him ask of God, etc." The promise is made to the one who lacks wisdom, not the one who has it. It is made to the one who realizes the limitations of his own wisdom and realizes his dependence on God for His wisdom. It is at this point that many alcoholics fail of guidance. They have such confidence in their own opinions, in their own judgment, and in their own ability to decide the course that they should pursue. They may (as a formality) ask God for His guidance, however, not really understand any deep sense of their need of His guidance. They may have such confidence in their own wisdom that they mistake their own judgment for the guidance of God. Having prayed for Wisdom, but still being confident in their own judgment, they become sure that their opinion is right and they attribute their own opinion to God. If we are to have God's guidance, we must release all confidence in our own judgment; and, in a sense of our own inability to decide for ourselves. We should come to God, putting our own notions aside, for Him to tell us what He would have us to do, and we should wait silently before Him to make known His will.

The *third step* toward obtaining Divine guidance is that we really desire to know God's will, and are thoroughly willing to do it whatever it may be. This also comes out in the promise. It reads, "If any of you lacks wisdom let him ask of God." Of course, the asking must be genuine, and there is no genuine asking wisdom of God unless we are eagerly desirous of knowing God's will and heartily willing to do it when that will is made known. The genuine and absolute surrender of the will to God is the great secret of guidance. The promise, "I will instruct you and teach you in the way you should go; I will guide you with My eye," (Psalms 32:8) as is evident from the context, is made to the one whose will is surrendered to God. The next verse reads, "Do not be like the horse *or* like the mule, *Which* have no understanding, Which must be harnessed with bit and bridle, Else they will not come near you." (Psalm 32:9)

God's instruction, teaching and guidance, His gentle guidance "with His eye upon us," is for the one whose will is entirely surrendered to Him. The surrender must be real surrender. There are many who think they know, but, what they are really seeking is to get God to say yes to their own plans. They are trying to get God to endorse the plan they themselves have already subconsciously formed, and they are not waiting, as they suppose they are, until God tells them what His will really is. They are waiting until God tells them to do the thing that they want to do and, in their subconscious self, have made up their mind to do, so they think and think and think, and pray and pray and pray, until they think themselves into thinking that God tells them to do the thing that they themselves wished to do from the outset.

The thing that they wanted to do from the outset may not be God's plan at all. This is one of the most frequent causes of thinking we have when we are only doing the thing that we want to do. Men and women who go to God for guidance in this way (i.e. without having absolutely put aside their own will and their own opinion), are the most positive in saying that God told them to do this and that. If we would be guided of God, we must make absolutely sure that we have put away our own will entirely and are willing to and desirous of doing God's will, whatever it may be.

We must be sure that we are silent before God and truly listening to His voice, and not still listening to this desire that we have in the depths of our heart that God shall tell us to do the thing that we want to do. When former friends asked me to go out with them for an evening, I went to God to show me what might be His will. There was a great conflict in my heart. There were reasons why I wished to go out that evening; there were reasons why I wished to stay away from the old scene, or why I thought I must stay at home. It took me two days to get absolutely silent before God, and to put away my own conflicting ideas on both sides. When I did come to the place where I had no will whatever in the matter, but simply wished to know God's will (whichever way it might be). When I became absolutely silent before God, He soon made the path in which He would have me go as plain as day.

The fact that the thing that we are contemplating doing is a hard thing and requires great sacrifice does not (by any means) make it definite that it is God's will and not ours. Our hearts naturally are deceitful above all things, and oftentimes willful persons will set their heart on doing a very hard thing. They may set their heart on doing it out of spiritual pride, or for many other reasons than because of surrender to the will of God. They want to do this hard thing, and they continuously pray, until they make themselves think that this hard thing is the will of God. It is very likely the thing that God would have them do is some basic, everyday sort of a thing. The best thing is God's will, whether that will be in a quiet life at home, or whether it be a notable life of courage and self-sacrifice in sharing a recovered life from alcoholism. If we are to have God's guidance, we must, become absolutely silent before God, and be willing and glad to serve Him in the most ordinary sort of life. It must be a life that seems far beneath our talents and our training, if that be His will, just as ready to do that as to serve Him in a field that demands large abilities and great sacrifice. Satan cheats many of God's children out of accomplishing the things that God would have them do by making them restless in the homely paths of doing things that they can do. He sets their heart on doing things that they cannot do; and they leave the path of actual achievement to brood over things they would like to do, but which it is not

God's will for them to do, and which they never will do. Oftentimes a whole life is wasted in this way.

The *fourth step* toward obtaining God's guidance is definite prayer for that guidance. "If any of you lacks wisdom," says God, "let him ask of God." There should be definite prayer for definite guidance. We should ask God's guidance at every turn of life; we should ask His guidance not merely in the great crises of life, but in the ordinary matters of everyday life—in our business, domestic work, and in the simplest things. None of us knows enough to direct our own steps in the simplest matters of every day life. We need God's guidance at every turn of life, and we can have it if we ask for it. Moreover, the asking will do no good unless we have already taken the other steps that have been mentioned. The definite prayer is the fourth step and not the first, and we should be sure we have taken the first three steps before we take the fourth.

The *fifth step* toward obtaining God's guidance is positive expectation that God will grant our prayer and gives us the guidance that we ask. This also comes out in the exact wording of the promise. It reads, "If any of you lacks wisdom, let him ask of God, who gives to all liberally and without reproach, and it will be given to him. But let him ask in faith, with no doubting, for he who doubts is like a wave of the sea driven and tossed by the wind. For let not that man (i.e., the man that doubts, the man who does not confidently expect) suppose that he will receive anything from the Lord." (James 1:5-7) Here is where many miss God's guidance. Their wills are surrendered, they really desire to know and do His will, and they ask God for His guidance, but they do not confidently expect that God will give the guidance they ask. They hope He will, but they are not sure that He will. If we have taken the other steps, when we ask God for His guidance we may be absolutely sure that God will give it. Someone may say, "But others have asked God's guidance and thought they had it, when the situation showed they did not. I may also be mistaken." No, not if you have taken the other steps already mentioned and will take the steps that I am still to mention. We have God's absolute promise of guidance made to those who meet the conditions which we have described, and therefore we may ask guidance with the absolute certainty that we are going to receive it. When we ask for God's wisdom, if we are of those to whom the promise is made, we know that we have asked something according to God's will, for He has definitely promised it in His Word. Therefore, we have a right to know that our prayer is heard and the thing we have asked is granted. (1 John 5:14,15)

I was recently speaking to a group of people on recovering from Alcoholism and living an abundant life, and as I left the platform to go to another engagement on a military base, I found the next speaker waiting for me on the outside of the audience. He was greatly excited. He was a gifted teacher of the Word of God and had been much used of God. He stopped me as I passed by hurrying to the train and said, "I am going to tear to pieces everything you have said to these young men." I replied, "If I have not spoken according to the Book I hope you will tear it to pieces, but what did I say that was not according to the Bible?" He answered, "Those alcoholics now have the impression that they can ask God to cure them from alcoholism and receive it." I replied, "I do not know whether that is the impression I produced or not, but that is the impression that I was aiming for." "But," he said, "That is wrong. We have twelve-step programs, counselors, and other programs that are beneficial." "Yes," I replied, "They are beneficial, however I recommend using them to gain as much information as possible about alcohol and its affects. God has revealed His will of us being healed and living life more abundantly." He made no reply. What reply was there to make? Here we have a definite promise of God; and, if we meet the conditions of that promise, we can be absolutely sure, that God will do as He says. Yes, absolutely sure that God will give us wisdom in any specific case in which we ask it. We should rest absolutely on God's plain promise, and when we ask to be cured from alcoholism, be absolutely sure that a cure is coming.

The *sixth step* toward obtaining God's guidance is to follow His guidance a step at a time as He gives it. Here again is where many recovering alcoholics miss their way. Many seek to know the whole way before they take a single step, but God's method is to show us a step at a time. Look at Peter in Acts 12. God led him a step at a time. First, the angel smote Peter on the side, awoke him, and then told him to arise up quickly.

Peter did it, and his chains fell from his hands. Then the angel said to him, "Gird thyself and bind on thy sandals," and he did so. Then the angel said to him, "Gird yourself and tie on your sandals"; and so he did. And he said to him, "Put on your garment and follow me" (Acts 12:8) Peter did exactly as he was told. He was not even sure that he was awake, but he followed step by step, even when he thought he might be asleep. They passed the first and second guard and came to the iron gate that led into the city. Peter did not stop and argue as to whether the gate would be opened or not, but just followed up to the gate, and when he got to the gate the gate opened of its own accord. God led him step by step, and so does God leads us. The Word of God tells us that "The steps of a *good* man are ordered by the LORD, And He delights in his way." (Psalm 37:23) The trouble with many of us is we wish God to show us the whole path, and are not willing to go a step at a time.

Step-by-step the Spirit will lead you, and step-by-step you must follow. The thing for us to do is to take the next step that God shows us in answer to our prayer and not wait until God shows us the whole way. Just continue on as God leads you, and He will show you what to do next. A very large share of our perplexity about the will of God is of this kind. We are troubled because God has not shown us what He wants us to do next year, or it may be next month. All we need is God's guidance for today. Follow His step-by-step program as He leads you. Just as He did with me, the way will open as you go.

The *seventh and final step* in the path that leads to God's sure guidance is that we must always bear in mind that God's guidance is clear guidance. Here is where many give up. They have impulses, but do not know from what source. They have what appear to be leadings, for example, to do something, but they are not sure it is God's leading. Very likely it is not God's leading; and yet they follow it for fear they may be disobeying God, or, perhaps they do not follow it and then get into condemnation—disobeying God. I have met many in the deepest gloom from this cause. They had an impression they ought to do a certain thing, they were not at all clear the impression was from God, they did not do the thing, and then the devil has made them think that they have disobeyed God, and some even think they have committed the unpardonable sin because they did not obey this prompting (of the origin of which they were not at all sure). If we will only bear in mind that God's guidance is clear guidance we will be delivered from this snare of Satan (the deliverer of alcohol). Satan will prevent drinkers making a full surrender to God just as long as he can, but when they do make a full surrender, and then the devil will do everything in his power to torment them. He will suggest all kinds of ridiculous things for them to do, and then they will not do them and Satan will torment them by making them think they have gone back on their surrender to God. Let us never forget that not all spiritual impressions are from the Holy Spirit. There are other spirits beside the Holy Spirit and we need to try the spirits whether they be of God. "Beloved, do not believe every spirit, but test the spirits, whether they are of God; because many false prophets have gone out into the world." (1 John 4:1) Some people are so anxious to be led of the Holy Spirit that they are willing to be led by any spirit and plunge into the delusions of spiritualism or other forms of fanaticism. I repeat it again, God's guidance is clear guidance and we should not follow any impression until God makes it as clear that it is from Him.

The main point in the whole matter of guidance is the absolute surrender of the will to God, the delighting in His will and the being willing to do joyfully the very things we would not like to do naturally.

God loves us and will guide us with His counsel to the end of our earthly pilgrimage, and afterwards receive us into glory. (Psalm 73:24)

As a boy, I was told by my parents that "For God so loved the world that He gave His only begotten Son, that whoever believes in Him should not perish but have everlasting life." (John 3:16) I was also told how Christ came to give us a more abundant life than we have, a life abundant in love (and therefore abundant in salvation for ourselves) and large in enterprise for the alleviation and redemption of the world.

To love abundantly is to live abundantly, and to love forever is to live forever. Hence, eternal life is inextricably bound up with love. We want to live forever for the same reason that we want to live tomorrow. Why do you want to live tomorrow? It is because there our God who loves you, and whom you want to be guided by, be with, and love back. There is no other reason why we should live, other than that we love and are beloved. Eternal life also is to know God, and God is love. This is Christ's own definition. Ponder it, "And this is life eternal, that they might know thee the only true God, and Jesus Christ, whom thou hast sent." (John 17:3) Love must be eternal. It is what God is. He wants you to live life more abundantly, therefore choose God because He loves you.

7

BUT JESUS MADE WINE!

Some people may argue that alcohol (or wine) is in the Bible and there is no problem in drinking it; because after all, Jesus made it.

First, allow me to present this narrative:

Jesus was at a wedding feast, and when the wine ran short, he provided more. "Jesus said to them, 'Fill the waterpots with water.' And they filled them up to the brim." (John 2:7) I do not think that I should do any good if I were to enter on the discussion as to what sort of wine our Lord Jesus made on this occasion. It was wine, and I am sure it was very good wine, for He would produce nothing but the best. Was it wine such as we understand it today? That which went under the name of wine was not true wine, but a fiery, brandied concoction of which I feel sure that Jesus would not have tasted a drop. The methods of modern wine manufacturers are very different from the juice of the grape, mildly exhilarating, which was the usual wine of times centuries passed. Had our great Exemplar lived under our present circumstances, surrounded by a sea of deadly drink, which is ruining tens of thousands, I know how he would have acted. I am sure he would not have contributed by word or deed to the rivers of poisonous beverages in which bodies and souls are now being destroyed wholesale. The kind of wine which he made was such that, if there had been no stronger drink in the world, nobody might have thought it necessary to enter any protest against drinking it. It would have done no harm to anyone, be sure of that, or else Jesus our loving Savior would not have made it.

Yes, Jesus said to them, "Fill the waterpots with water."

There is profitable reading in the Scriptures. Search the Scriptures. Search them as much as you can. Try to understand them. You may be thinking, "But if I know the Bible, will I be saved?" No, you must know Christ himself by the Spirit. While you are studying the Scriptures you may expect the Savior will bless His own word, and guide you.

In the New Testament we deal mainly with one word—wine. It comes into the New Testament with the double duty of representing both the generic (for all kinds of wine in the Old Testament) and the specific (for unfermented wine). Since it was never used to render intoxicating wine, the presumption is therefore that in the New Testament it should never be made to stand for fermented wine. Let us now examine those New Testament texts where wine occurs, and inquire what the testimony of this word is, "New wine in old bottles." (Twice: Matt. 9:17; Mark 2:22; Luke 5:37, 38) The adjective "new" introduced into these texts supports the idea that wine is commonly used as a generic. The word "new" makes its meaning specific. The new and old used in these passages are figures of the new and old dispensations, and cannot be used in any way as putting the Savior's approval on the use of wine. Contrary to most arguments that Jesus made intoxicating wine, read the following scriptures: (all King James Versions)

"Gave Him to drink wine mingled with myrrh."   (Mark 15: 23)

"John the Baptist came neither eating bread nor   (Luke 7:33, 34)
drinking wine."

"The Good Samaritan poured in oil and wine."   (Luke 10:34)

"It is good neither to eat flesh nor to drink wine." (Romans 14:21)

"Not given to much wine." (Deacons)   (1 Timothy 3:8)

"Drink a little wine for thy stomach's sake."   (1 Timothy 5:23)

"Not given to much wine." (Aged women)   (Titus 2:3)

"See that thou hurt not the oil and the wine."   (Revelation 6:6)

"Jesus turned water into wine."   (John 2:3; 4:46)

If there is but one kind of wine mentioned anywhere in Scripture, and if that is always intoxicating, then Jesus turned water into intoxicating wine. However, if that be true, then fermented or intoxicating wine is a proper beverage for everyone. On the other hand, there are two kinds of wine constantly referred to in the Old Testament, one of them fermented and the other unfermented. Now, the questions arise, which kind did Jesus make? Did He make intoxicating wine, which is everywhere condemned and forbidden in the Old Testament? Or did he make non-intoxicating wine, which is everywhere blessed and commended in the Old Testament? All a person needs is common sense and ordinary honesty to see that Jesus could not have made a drink which the Bible everywhere condemns and prohibits.

Therefore, it is preposterous to say that Christ made, that Paul recommended, and that the deacons and aged women used intoxicating wine. What Jesus did make and what Paul did recommend to Timothy was non-intoxicating wine, which always (and everywhere) has the divine smile and blessing on it.

Only once in the New Testament is wine spoken of with disapprobation. It also carried a qualifying term with it, which makes it certain that the word is not used in the ordinary or generic sense, but in a specific sense. For intoxicating wine, "And do not be drunk with wine, in which is dissipation; but be filled with the Spirit." (Ephesians 5:18) The word is also used figuratively seven times in the Book of Revelation: "Wine of the wrath of God," etc.

To make it still more certain that the New Testament writers never use the single word wine as a specific term for intoxicating wine, let it be observed that whenever they speak of wine that is intoxicating, they always resort to the use of other words than wine. For such purpose we have two other words, each used but once in the New Testament:

"For he will be great in the sight of the Lord, and shall drink neither wine nor strong drink ..." (Luke 1:15)

What has already been said is quite sufficient to show that the entire Bible is squarely on the side of total abstinence, and unqualifiedly opposed to the beverage use of all intoxicating liquors. There are also many general declarations of Scripture which forbid wine-drinking and condemn drunkenness in most vigorous and uncompromising language. Among them are these:

"Wine *is* a mocker, Strong drink *is* a brawler, And whoever is led astray by it is not wise." (Proverbs 20:1) Truly wine is a past-master in the art of deception. Just think of the millions of deluded souls that it has ruined!

"Who has woe? Who has sorrow? Who has contentions? Who has complaints? Who has wounds without cause? Who has redness of eyes? Those who linger long at the wine, Those who go in search of mixed wine. Do not look on the wine when it is red, When it sparkles in the cup, *When* it swirls around smoothly; At the last it bites like a serpent, And stings like a viper." (Proverbs 23:29-32)

"Woe to those who rise early in the morning, *That* they may follow intoxicating drink; Who continue until night, *till* wine inflames them!" (Isaiah 5:11)

"Woe to him who gives drink to his neighbor, Pressing *him to* your bottle, Even to make *him* drunk, That you may look on his nakedness! You are filled with shame instead of glory. You also—drink! And be exposed as uncircumcised! The cup of the LORD's right hand *will be* turned against you, And utter shame will be on your glory." (Habakkuk 2:15-16)

"Do not mix with winebibbers, *Or* with gluttonous eaters of meat; For the drunkard and the glutton will come to poverty, And drowsiness will clothe *a man* with rags." (Proverbs 23:20-21)

"Now the works of the flesh are evident, which are: adultery, fornication, uncleanness, lewdness, idolatry, sorcery, hatred, contentions, jealousies, outbursts of wrath, selfish ambitions, dissensions, heresies, envy, murders, drunkenness, revelries, and the like; of which I tell you beforehand, just as I also told *you* in time past, that those who practice such things will not inherit the kingdom of God. But the fruit of the Spirit is love, joy, peace, longsuffering, kindness, goodness, faithfulness, gentleness, self-control. Against such there is no law." (Galatians 5: 19-23)

In conclusion, this is practically the whole case as the wine question appears in the Sacred Scriptures, and it seems strange that any person can find in these records one word that favors the use of fermented wine as a beverage or that anywhere puts the divine endorsement on the use of intoxicating drink of any kind. Total abstinence from the use of all intoxicating beverages is clearly the teaching of the Word of God. To abstain is the solemn injunction everywhere. Therefore, whoever persists in the use of strong drink does it in defiance of the solemn warnings and positive prohibitions of the Word of God. That individual's eternal life is at stake.

8

WINNING THE FIGHT!

After reading the first six chapters of this book, many unfortunate alcoholics says, "I will arise, and go to my father." They go to the Father through Jesus. They are the promise of abundant pardon. They look into the face of God and cry, "Though he slay me, yet will I trust Him." They learn that the Lord is near to those that are of a broken heart, and He saves those of a contrite spirit. They hear the voice of God affirming that "For *whoever calls on the name of the LORD shall be saved.*" (Romans 10:13) They call on the Lord. The precious gift of saving faith is given to them. No longer relying on themselves (or anyone else), knowing at last that justification has come by God's grace, through the redemption that is in Jesus Christ.

When poor drunkards throw themselves on God, salvation is at hand! Those who seek release from alcohol or any other besetting sin know that they are saved. They know it because those that believe on the Son of God has the witness in himself that they have entered among those who are sanctified through the offering of the body of Jesus Christ once for all. They know it because as "For by one offering He has perfected forever those who are being sanctified," (Hebrews 10:14) so "*This is the covenant that I will make with them after those days, says the LORD: I will put My laws into their hearts, and in their minds I will write them,"* then He adds, *"Their sins and their lawless deeds I will remember no more."* (Hebrews 10:16) They know it as I know it, by personal experience and daily observation. They know it because they fully realize that "Therefore, if anyone *is* in Christ, *he is* a new creation; old things have passed away; behold, all things have become new." (2 Corinthians 5:17)

Yes, as alcoholics, once slaves of alcohol, but now a child of God, goes forth, hearkening to the voice of the Spirit which whispers, "Fear not, for I *am* with you; Be not dismayed, for I *am* your God. I will strengthen you, Yes, I will help you, I will uphold you with My righteous right hand" (Isaiah 41:10) they know that God's keeping power is as omnipotent as His saving power. He will remove the taste from their mouths. Most people acquire a taste for liquor which results in the disease of drunkenness, primarily to get away from some condition in their lives. Actually, very few have a natural liking for alcohol. All through life, the story is the same—just an effort to get away from oneself. The overworked individual seeks to conquer the sense of fatigue after the long day with a beer or two. The businessperson beset with corporate troubles separates themselves from their troubles for a few hours by indulging in a half dozen stiff cocktails. The unhappy married couple seeks a remedy a recent fight with a night out at the club.

Last of all, the confirmed drunkard (above all others) seeks to efface himself for a few hours from his pitiable condition. I have examined, not hundreds, but thousands of cases, and in every one a few simple questions located the underlying cause of the disease. Ambition, restlessness, over-strain, unhappiness and anything that tends to dissatisfaction with one's status in life are all among the prime excitants to drinking.

My plea is to let alcohol stand by itself. If alcohol could be shown in all its nakedness (as the universal scourge of all mankind), public opinion would rise to such a height that the seeming power of alcohol could not withstand it.

There must be drunkenness among the officers and men of the Navy or there would be no necessity for the proclamation to deglamorize alcohol. What is to become of the Navy drunkard? I was that drunkard! Now, I am saved. I used the advice stamped on government printed funds, "In God We Trust." Yes, in God I trusted and He delivered me from alcoholism. He saved me and if you trust Him, He will save you.

I read that an ex-governor made the statement, "I am not now and never was a drunkard, but I have been drunk."

Well, a person may say, "I am not now and never was a murderer, but I have committed murder," or "I am not now and never was a forger, but I have committed forgery." We should be honest with ourselves. We cannot fool the public through self-deception. I was a drunkard. I am now an ex-drunkard, not a reformed drunkard. You cannot make imperfection into perfection.

"Who can bring a clean *thing* out of an unclean? No one!" (Job 14:4)

Let us not take likely the plain fact of today. Let us consider a special class of people who have contact with this liquor question. This class is composed of those who have convictions and the courage to express them.

These are they who turn neither to the right nor to the left; who walk straight on through a mass of staggering men, frantic women, and children diseased or disgraced. They are searching for something that will end it all. They search for something that will take the stagger out of the alcoholic's legs, the blear out of the eye, the trembling out of the hand, the stench out of the breath. These people with the purpose of discovering a remedy for all this debasement of the spirit and destruction of the body make no compromise.

Navy policy has forbidden the use of any form of alcoholic drink (to both officers and crew) on our warships.

Think of it!

But let us suppose that alcohol is wiped out in a wholesale outburst of public indignation. What then? Will that change human character and nature? Will it alter the impulses, the ambitions or the instincts that guide our actions? Will it wipe away unrest, overstrain or unhappiness? Will it banish that terrible desire to *get away from oneself?* I have major doubts. And unless it does, alcoholics who have escaped from one (and have not sought God for healing) will seek some other strong agent to do for them what alcohol did.

In my own case, ceasing to drink was the smallest part of my salvation. Christian living alone made me immune from the varied temptations of life.

In the human sense, I was a drunkard for a period of years. I can truthfully say that the real Anthony Parker, God's spiritual man (made in His image and after His likeness) never was, never can be, and never will be a drunkard. My body was drunk for twenty-three years, but the body is not I, but mine.

Drunkenness will exist, legislation or no legislation, license or no license, prohibition or no prohibition, local option or no local option, until men and women realize that their bodies are not themselves but theirs, and learn that divine Mind alone controls them. How can men and women learn this? The answer is: Through the teaching and the understanding of the Bible. When alcoholics are healed of drunkenness through most programs, no effort is made to truly change their thoughts and no claim is made that their thoughts have been changed.

Becoming a Christian not only heals them of drunkenness, but destroys all physical sense of discord. It causes them to seek an abundant life equal to Christian thinking.

Someone once said that the nation could not survive half drunk and half sober. I add that a man or woman cannot succeed half bad and half good. Alcoholics who are healed of alcoholism and continues in the old way of thinking, looking on drunkenness with gratification and abstaining from it through fear of the consequences is living half bad and half good.

"I know your works, that you are neither cold nor hot. I could wish you were cold or hot. So then, because you are lukewarm, and neither cold nor hot, I will vomit you out of My mouth." (Revelation 3:15-16)

Why do men and women drink? I say, "To get away from themselves." Liquor only gives them a temporary sense of relief from their troubles. Christian living provides the remedy which the alcoholic seeks erroneously.

Through this healing, the desire to drink is destroyed and none of them are healed until this is done. Man does not leave drunkenness. Drunkenness leaves him.

Christian healing, whether in drunkenness or any other disease, finds that our being, our existence is spiritual. Spiritual man was demonstrated by Jesus when He rose from the dead, or rather, when He showed that what was called death had no power. Only a spiritual being could do this, could come back from the grave.

Therefore if man's nature is spiritual, he must be subject only to spiritual laws and conditions, not to physical laws and conditions.

Again, if man is subject only to spiritual laws and conditions, any material or physical remedy or treatment must necessarily be wholly outside the domain of his existence and therefore ineffective.

What then is this alcoholism for which we seek a cure? It is trying to heal the physical person only, and this belief or claim includes the alcohol, the temptation to drink, the drunkard, and that which sees, knows, and condemns the alcohol and the alcoholic.

To heal and fully recover from alcoholism begins with Jesus Christ. We see that Jesus Christ is the Healer in all cases, and that Christian treatment means that the practitioner is constantly looking away from the senses to his own and his patient's refuge, the eternal God, which is too pure to behold iniquity.

God's treatment, unlike all other forms of treatment, does not deal at all with personality. It defines perfection and imperfection showing that one is, and one is not, the Truth. Truth makes alcoholics free from the illusion that there is, was, or will be any power apart from the Mind which Christ Jesus proved to be true. Christian healing means eternal salvation in which there is no power to sin or be sick and where one person is never the superior of another. It is where God wipes away all tears and we love our neighbor as ourselves.

The difference between the Christian's treatment of alcoholism and other forms of treatment is the difference between "do" and "done." The Christian's treatment finds that all is done and done perfectly. Other treatments seek to change imperfection into perfection which is impossible. Jesus says, "Most assuredly, I say to you, he who hears My word and believes in Him who sent Me has everlasting life, and shall not come into judgment, but has passed from death into life." (John 5:24)

Our Lord desires that we *might have it more abundantly*. Literally, He is saying that we may have *abundance*, or that which abounds. The word denotes that which is not absolutely essential to *life*, but which is superadded to make life happy. You will not merely have *life*—simple, bare *existence*—but you will have all those superadded things which are needful to make your life eminently blessed and happy. Jesus will give you eternal joy, peace, the society of the blessed, and all those exalted means of felicity which are prepared for you in the world of glory if you trust Him.

AFTERWORD

Many have said that this book starts out rather, warmly and wound up most abundantly. I had a run with alcohol spanning twenty-three years. I know all about drinking. I figured it this way: I will lose in efficiency, even if I keep my health. Being selfish and perhaps getting sensible, I desire the remaining productive years of my life to be years of the greatest efficiency. Looking back over my drinking years, I saw that it was my duty if I was to attain and keep that greatest efficiency. It could not be complicated with any alcohol-fighting whatsoever.

I decided that what I might lose in the companionship and social end of it I would gain in my own personal increase in horsepower. I knew that though drinking may have *appeared* to have done me no physical harm, it certainly did me no good. If I had persisted, it surely would have done me harm in some way or another.

So, I held a caucus with myself. I called myself into convention and discussed the proposition some-what like this:

"You are now over forty years of age. You are sound physically and you are no weaker mentally than you have always been, so far as can be discovered by the outside world. You have had a lot of fun, much of it complicated with the conviviality that comes with drinking and much of it not so complicated. You have done your share of plain and fancy drinking, and it has not killed you yet. There is absolutely no nutriment in being dead. That gets you nothing save a few obituary notices you will never see. There is even less in being sick and peddling around in everybody's way. It is as sure as sunset, if you continue on your present road, that alcohol will destroy you just as it has destroyed a lot of other people you know and knew. There are two methods of procedure open to you. One is to keep it up and continue having the fun you think you are having and take what is inevitably coming to you. The other is to turn your life over to God, so that you can fully recover and be healed and live the rest of your years more abundantly."

I viewed it from every angle I could think of. I thought I would have a hard job laid out before me if I quit. I weighed the whole thing in my mind in the light of my acquaintances, experiences, position, style of life, and feelings. I had been through it many times. I had often gone on the waterwagon for periods varying in length from three days to three months. I was not venturing into any uncharted territory. I knew every signpost, crossroad, foot of the ground. I knew the difficulties—knew them by heart. I was not deluding myself with any assertions of superior willpower, superior courage or superior anything. I knew I had a fixed daily habit of drinking, and that if I quit drinking I would have to reorganize my entire life. However, this time it would be different. I asked and trusted God to restore and heal me. He saved me through faith in His ability.

You must believe that Christ saves His people from sin through faith; that Christ's Spirit is received by faith to dwell in the heart. It is faith that works by love. By faith, Christians overcome the world, the flesh, the Devil, and even mighty Alcohol. It is by faith that we quench the fiery darts of the wicked. It is by faith that we put on the Lord Jesus Christ and put off the old person. It is by faith that we fight the good fight and "stand." This is the victory that overcomes the world, even our faith. It is by faith that our flesh is kept under carnal desires subdued by Alcoholism. The fact is that it is simply by faith that we receive the Spirit of Christ to work in us to will and to do, according to His good pleasure.

Jesus Christ sheds abroad His own love in our hearts, and thereby enkindles ours. Every victory over sin is by faith in Christ; and whenever the mind is diverted from Christ (by resolving and fighting against sin), whether we are aware of it or not, we are acting in our own strength, rejecting the help of Christ, and are under a specious delusion. Nothing but the life and energy of the Spirit of Christ within us can save us from sin, and trust is the uniform and universal condition of the working of this saving energy within us. We must learn one of the hardest lessons of the human heart—to renounce self-dependence and trust wholly in Christ.

Sizing it up, one side against the other, I conclude that it is better for me not to drink. I find I have much more time that I can devote to living life more abundantly. I think more clearly, feel better, do not make any loose statements under the exhilaration of alcohol, and keep my mind on helping others take back their lives. The concept of time is a lofty one. It is astonishing how much time you have to do things. When you are drinking, you are never too busy to take a drink and never too busy not to stop. You are busy all the time but get nowhere. Work is the curse of the drinking classes. Anyone who has been accustomed to do the kind of drinking I did for twenty-three years, who likes the sociability and the companionship of it, will find that the sudden transition to a non-drinking life will leave a new and exciting existence.

I leave you to look directly at Jesus Christ through the Gospel and by an act of loving trust. You can say this simple prayer and be on your way to a life filled with abundance.

Dear Heavenly Father,

I come to You in the name of Jesus. I am so sorry for my sins and the alcoholic life I have lived. Please forgive me and cleanse me with Your blood from all unrighteousness. In Romans 10:9, you said if we confess the Lord our God and believe in our hearts that God raised Him from the dead, we shall be saved. Well, Father, I confess Jesus Christ as the Lord of my soul. With my heart and mind, I believe You raised Him from the dead. This very moment I accept Jesus Christ as my own personal Savior and right now I am saved. I confess that I am healed and whole, mentally, physically, emotionally and spiritually. I ask that you remove all taste of alcohol from me. Thank You, Jesus, for dying for me and giving me eternal life. Amen

RESOURCES

Learn the signs of Alcoholism; obtain information on alcohol, including treatment and referral, professional intervention, and contact information from the following resources:

Internet

Soberrecovery.com
Addict-help.com
LifeScript.com
Addictionresourceguide.com
Mtregis.com
GetAlcoholismHelp.com
Alcohol-rehab.net
Angelfire.com
Alcoholismresources.com
Ama-assn.org
Alcoholism.about.com
Addiction.lovetoknow.com/wiki/Alcoholism_Resources

Christian-based Treatment

Pacific Hills Treatment Centers, Inc.	1-866-330-1482	pachills.com
Grace Track for Christians	1-800-781-6113	gracetrack.net
Calvary Ranch	1-800-404-2258	calvaryranch.org
Alcoholics for Christ	1-800-441-7877	alcoholicsforchrist.com
Goal Ministries International	1-888-229-3045	goalproject.org
His Mansion Ministries	1-603-464-5555	hismansion.com

Christian Recovery Library

alcoholicsvictorious.org

978-0-595-49683-9
0-595-49683-0